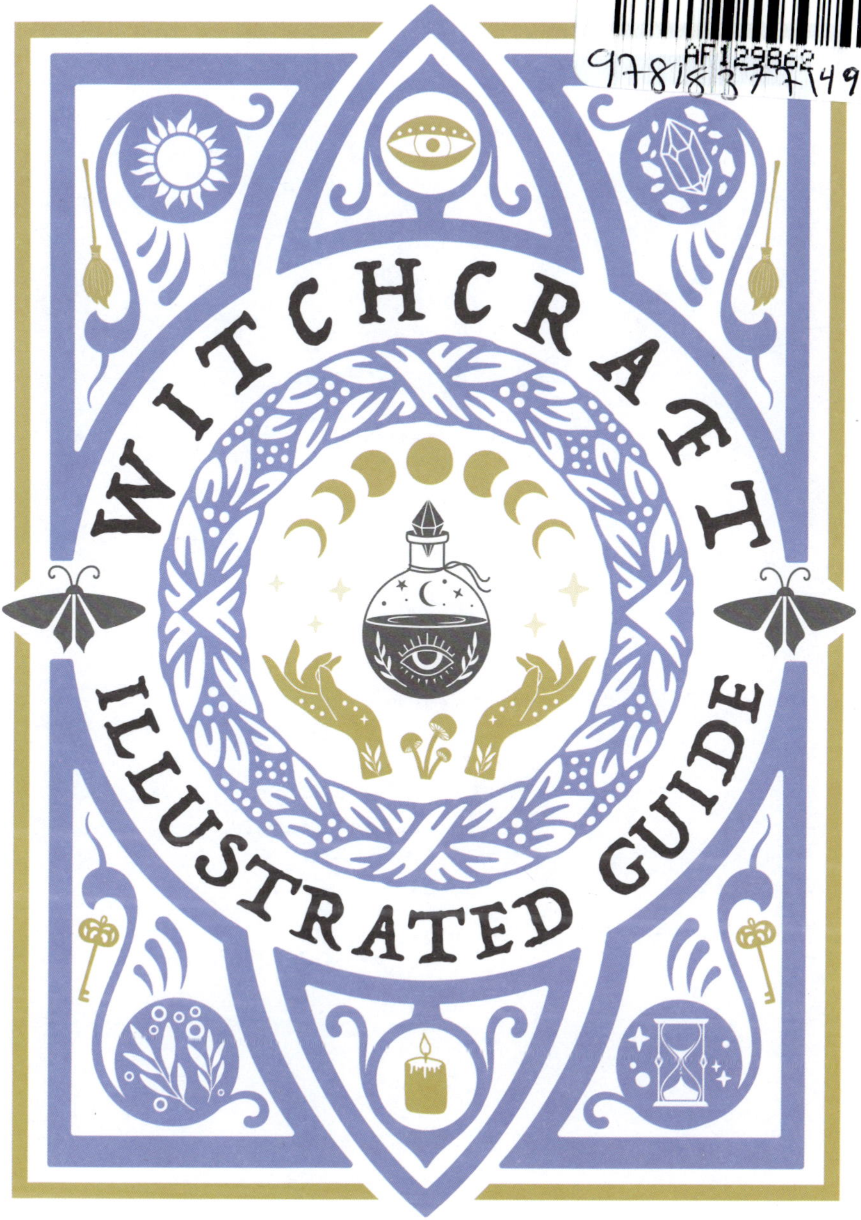

WITCHCRAFT
ILLUSTRATED GUIDE

Designed by Simon Parker
Edited by Cameron-Rose Neal

Copyright © 2023 Igloo Books Ltd

Published in 2024
First published in the UK by SparkPool Publishing
An imprint of Igloo Books Ltd
Cottage Farm, NN6 0BJ, UK
Owned by Bonnier Books
Sveavägen 56, Stockholm, Sweden

All rights reserved, including the right of reproduction
in whole or in part in any form.

Manufactured in China. 0524 002
10 9 8 7 6 5 4 3 2 1

Library of Congress Cataloging-in-Publication
Data is available upon request.

ISBN 978-1-83771-493-3
igloobooks.com
bonnierbooks.co.uk

CONTENTS

TIME TO START YOUR MAGICAL JOURNEY!........................ 4

CHARMS, TALISMANS, AFFIRMATIONS, INCANTATIONS............10

HOW TO CHOOSE AND ACTIVATE YOUR CRYSTALS 12

THE MAGIC IN COLOR AND DAYS.. 14

DRESSING AND ANOINTING THE CANDLE 16

BUILDING THE GRIMOIRE..18

INTRODUCTION TO SPELLS AND INCANTATIONS 20

SPELLS FOR HEALTH AND WELLNESS..22

SPELLS FOR PEACE AND HAPPINESS 28

SPELLS FOR POWER AND PROTECTION 34

SPELLS FOR FRIENDS AND FAMILY... 42

SPELLS FOR LOVE AND SEX 50

SPELLS FOR WEALTH AND PROSPERITY 58

WITCHCRAFT LEXICON/INDEX 64

TIME TO START YOUR MAGICAL JOURNEY!

In its true sense, witchcraft is a collection of beliefs in the supernatural that dates back centuries, if not thousands of years. It includes traditions and practices that involve using magic to bring about desired outcomes.

Introduction

When you think of witches, does your mind conjure images of cauldrons, cats, and black, pointed hats? Do you imagine elderly women with hooked noses and warts? While deeply ingrained in our collective consciousness, these images are outdated, out of sync with the times, and a little radical! In the modern world, witchcraft has taken on a vibrant new look. Imbued with positivity, people are embracing witchcraft and reclaiming the skills that possess an ancient history. It's time to replace the outdated images which spring to mind with pictures of powerful men and women, working potent magic—without a cape or broomstick in sight (though, there may still be a cat or two!).

Today, witchcraft has taken on a fresh feel and positive outlook. Modern witches are turning to salts, crystals, oils, and spells to enhance their lives. By embracing non-traditional forms of spirituality and utilizing underestimated skills of intuition and emotional intelligence, these witches are channeling the craft in its purest form.

Starting the Journey

Witchcraft embodies a common desire to bring positivity into the world using magic. Stemming from a variety of origins, practices would often pay respect to Earth's elements. Representation of the natural elements is still prevalent in many of the spells you will encounter when beginning your magical journey. Using the ingredients listed in this book, you'll be able to start positively enhancing your life by working in harmony with universal energies to bring about beneficial events and outcomes. From protecting yourself with pink salt to finding inner peace with the use of essential oils and amethyst, you can begin to use your energy to enhance your career, relationships, economic power, home, well-being, and more. Join the witches around the world who are striving to become empowered, enriched, and able to bring about positive control and influence to their lives. Sound uplifting, magical, and daring? Sounds like witchcraft!

How to use this book

So, if you are interested in witchcraft and what it could do for you, get set to tap into this inspiring world. By using your natural talents and some real-world elements, you can learn to harness potent magic which can improve your life. This book will help you to manifest an improvement in your finances, your health, your relationships, and much more. You'll discover how to help others by connecting to your spirituality and inner power and learn how to bring about these changes.

A WITCH'S TOOLS

In your witch's kit, you'll find some of the key ingredients which will allow you to set out on your magical journey with ease. Using pink salt for a little bit of self-love and protection, amethyst chips for your crown chakra and third eye, and lavender oil to manifest and anoint, you're ready to begin casting! Once you're confident with these elements, you can begin to grow your store and try more of the spells in this collection.

Amethyst chips

Glass jar

Pink salt

Lavender essential oil

This book requires the use of essential oils, candles, smudging, and general use of open flames. Always use essential oils with care and consult a doctor if you suffer from any adverse effects. Please exercise caution when using open flames and ensure lit candles are never left unattended. When smudging or burning other items during spells, keep a fireproof tray or plate to hand and keep a close eye on them. Happy casting!

Setting up your altar

Every witch needs an altar of their own. An altar is a sacred place where you can go for healing, inspiration, spiritual rituals, spellwork, or just to recenter yourself after a stressful day. An altar is a place to put all your favorite meaningful and magical items on display, ready for enchantment any time they're needed. The size and shape of your altar does not matter—what matters is that it's your space and you feel good in it.

AN ALTAR OF YOUR OWN
Setting up an altar shouldn't be too difficult. First, choose a piece of furniture to use as an altar. You can repurpose or buy something new, use a small wall shelf, bedside table, or even a windowsill as an altar. Some people have a permanent altar, while others who have limited space might use a drawer or a shelf on a bookcase. If space is really tight, find a box to keep your magical objects safe and private, and take them out and place them on top of the box when in use. Make sure you can sit comfortably and quietly and, when choosing where to put your altar, trust your instincts. When a space feels right, you'll just know it in your witchy bones!

SACRED SET~UPS
Now for the really fun part—setting up your altar. Witches believe that it's important to incorporate the four elements of the universe that are essential to life—Earth, Air, Water, and Fire—into their practice. You could have stones, plants, or flowers to represent Earth; candles, incense, or oil burners to represent Fire; a bowl of water, seashells, or sea glass to represent Water, and a feather, wind chimes, or a diffuser to represent Air. The elements are also linked to different directions, so placement is important. Items linked to the Earth element should sit at north, Air at east, Fire at south, and Water at west.

OWN IT!
Your altar is your space; you can add anything that holds significance to you such as jewelry, charms, or books. You could hang a witch's ladder for good energy and protection above the altar, or drape fabric over the surface.

The witch's pantry

Any witch worth their salt has a pantry stocked with magical herbs, spices, incense, and oils, ready to use in a variety of spells and potions!

HERBS AND OTHER BOTANICALS

When you come across a spell which requires ingredients such as "botanicals," this just means a plant or a plant part, like flowers, leaves, seeds, stems, roots, etc. Herbs are plants such as rosemary, parsley, and so on, which are used for their flavor as well as their magical or medicinal properties.

ESSENTIAL OILS

Essential oils are highly concentrated extracts of flowers, herbs, roots, or resin extract, sometimes diluted in neutral-base oil. They're commonly used to anoint tools that are used in spells and rituals, such as candles and crystals. Some witches even use them to anoint their own bodies. Take care with oils and avoid using them around your eyes or on your skin. It's a good idea to keep clean cotton gloves in your witch's kitchen for handling sensitive materials.

INCENSE

Incense is a substance that contains fragrant herbs, flowers, resins, gums, and wood chips, infused with pure essential oils that you burn to release their scent. You can buy different blends of incense for different magical purposes, like a protection incense to drive away negative energies. You can also make your own blends.

Key ingredients

- **BAY:** for strength and prophetic dreams.
- **CHAMOMILE:** promotes inner peace, eases rage and heightened sensitivity, and invites luck and love.
- **CINNAMON:** use for love, passion, prosperity, personal strength, and psychic awareness.
- **CUMIN:** good for healing, protection, love, lust, new beginnings, and emotional strength.
- **GARLIC:** use for protection, strength, and healing.
- **GINGER:** use for healing, protection, luck, passion, and spell enhancement.
- **LAVENDER:** use for happiness, strengthening relationships, inner strength, psychic power, peace, and meditation.
- **ROSEMARY:** use for its strong protective, and cleansing powers.
- **SAGE:** use for wisdom, wishes, knowledge, strength, cleansing, and vitality.
- **THYME:** use for strength, courage, wisdom, and willpower in difficult situations.
- **EUCALYPTUS OIL:** invokes calmness, improves concentration, and promotes balance and healing.
- **MINT OIL:** cleansing and motivational.
- **GERANIUM OIL:** helps to decrease stress and balance emotions while calming and restoring inner peace.
- **CLOVE OIL:** protection, cleansing, spiritual healing, and spell enhancement.
- **ROSE OIL:** inspires emotional calm and stability.
- **PEPPERMINT OIL:** helps to soothe the nerves, focus the senses, and stimulate alertness.
- **LAVENDER OIL:** peace, dreams, relaxation, protection, banishing, and cleansing.
- **SANDALWOOD:** decreases anxiety, calms the nervous system and helps you sleep better.
- **DRAGON'S BLOOD:** use for protection, cleansing, purifying, and strengthening.
- **FRANKINCENSE:** reduces stress, helping to improve your mood and your concentration.
- **YLANG-YLANG:** enhances your inner confidence, filling you with warmth and joy.
- **PATCHOULI:** known for being sensual, grounding, and alluring.

CHARMS, TALISMANS, AFFIRMATIONS, INCANTATIONS

Your treasure trove of magical resources doesn't have to be limited to your altar. There are many other spellbinding objects and activities you can add to your witchy box of tricks. Words, feelings, and thoughts can bring about change in the physical world, too.

Charmed, I'm sure . . .

From four-leaf clovers to dice and horseshoes, lots of different things are traditionally used by people as lucky charms. A charm is an object that represents a change or result that you desire. Usually worn or carried, they may be kept in a pouch or purse or worn under clothes. They can be left in the home or other spaces to expel bad vibes or to be used when making magic. Almost any object can become a charm, as long as it means something to you and helps you to channel your energy to the world around you.

Some people wear their amulets and talismans. An amulet is a natural object used as a charm. Amulets can be things like stones, crystals, fossils, bird feathers, four-leaf clovers, pieces of wood, nuts, shells, dried flowers, or other herbs and seeds. You can choose any object that speaks to you for an amulet. Talismans are human-made objects that are used as a charm and are often carried by their owners at all times, typically on a chain around the neck. They may be made from materials found in nature and usually incorporate words or symbols.

Affirmative!

So much of what you'll do as a witch will come down to confidence and belief. Affirmations are powerful phrases you write down or memorize and then read out loud and repeat. They can be life changing. To choose a phrase, think about who you are, how you feel, and who you want to be, such as: "I can achieve anything I set out to do," or, "I am letting go of the past." At first, repeating a phrase might feel strange, silly, or even like a waste of time. Rest assured: it isn't. Words are powerful and affirmations can really help you harness the power of positive thinking and mindfulness, and channel your inner energy.

Incantations

An incantation is a spell created by using words and can be spoken, sung, or chanted. Incantations don't have to rhyme or be full of fancy words, but they need to be spoken like you mean them, which is why getting good at affirmations can help you to enhance your magical abilities.

HOW TO CHOOSE AND ACTIVATE YOUR CRYSTALS

Crystals are more than just pretty stones which beautify an altar (though, they do that, too!). Crystals are minerals which can absorb and direct energy; used for a variety of magical and healing purposes.

Charging and cleansing crystals

Before you can use crystals in spells, you need to activate or "charge" them with an intention. Be clear about what you need to achieve in your spell. Charge the crystal by filling it with the energy you feel during your visualization and think about what you want—anything from soothing a headache to finding a friend. Visualize the outcome as though it's already happened. How will you feel when your wish comes true? The more energy and enthusiasm you can put into this, the stronger the crystal's power will be.

Cleanse any new crystals you buy, are gifted or you use regularly to refresh them and remove any negative energy they've absorbed. Methods of cleansing crystals include placing them in a bowl of salt water, smudging them with sage smoke, or leaving them in direct sun or moonlight.

Types Of Crystals

AMETHYST is a purple stone that can protect from negative energy and help relieve stress and strain. It is also said to boost magical powers and help make people more aware of their surroundings.

CLEAR QUARTZ, as its name suggests, is all about clarity. It clears the mind, body, and spirit of any clutter and helps with concentration and memory.

ROSE QUARTZ is said to enhance all types of love, whether that be self-love, love for others, or unconditional love.

BLACK TOURMALINE is said to be able to soak up negative vibes and get rid of toxicity. It can also make you feel more grounded when life gets a bit much.

CITRINE is bright yellow and its cleansing properties can help when you're feeling stuck to restore good vibes and confidence.

JADE is green and brings good luck in money and relationships; said to help improve a sense of balance, stability, peace, and wisdom.

OBSIDIAN is a powerful volcanic crystal used for protection and to shield you against negativity.

THE MAGIC IN COLOR AND DAYS

In magic, colors and days have powers that can inform all of your spells and even your day-to-day life. To fully tune in to the power of colors, you need to know a bit more about their meanings. Then, you're all set to surround yourself with some color magic.

The power of color

These are the general meanings that colors hold, and what they represent magically, but we all relate to colors in different ways, so you may want to experiment to find what feels right for you.

RED: for strong emotions, courage, passion, and strength.
ORANGE: for energy, attraction, vibrancy, and motivation.
YELLOW: for inspiration, imagination, and knowledge.
GREEN: for growth, wealth, renewal, luck, and balance.
BLUE: for calm, truth, wisdom, and protection.
PURPLE: for spirituality, wisdom, devotion, peace, and idealism.
PINK: for nurturing, emotional healing, and harmony.
WHITE: for peace, innocence, understanding, and purity.
BLACK: for dignity, force, stability, protection, and repels negativity.
GOLD: for inner strength, self-realisation, understanding, good fortune, and intuition.
SILVER: for wisdom, psychic ability, intelligence, and memory.

Days of magic

Each of the seven days of the week carries its own magical energy and is linked to different colors. Learning these connections can help you choose the most auspicious time and hues to practice magic!

MONDAY is linked to silver, white, and blue: peace, beauty, sleep, dreams, emotions, travel, fertility, insight, and wisdom.
TUESDAY is linked to red, black, and orange: courage, strength, success, self-belief, rebellion, and self-defence.
WEDNESDAY is linked to purple and orange: communication, creativity, change, and good fortune.
THURSDAY is linked to blue and green: abundance, protection, strength, wealth, and healing.
FRIDAY is linked to pink and aqua: love, birth, fertility, romance, gentleness, and friendship.
SATURDAY is linked to black and purple: banishing, protection, wisdom, spirituality, and cleansing.
SUNDAY is linked to gold and yellow: success, promotion, wealth, and prosperity.

DRESSING AND ANOINTING THE CANDLE

Candles are a staple item in any witch's box of tricks and can be used in rituals and spells to increase and release energy. Associated with fire, they often represent transformation and can help you tap into this energy, as fire changes everything it touches.

Dressing a candle

Just as you need to charge a crystal to be able to use it in a magic spell or setting, you also need to charge a candle to instill it with magical intent and energy. This is known as "dressing" a candle. Before doing this, set aside some time when you won't be disturbed and find a quiet place, such as your altar, to do it. The more focused you can be, the stronger the intentions with which you will charge your candles.

1. First, research what kind of oils will support your spell.

2. Then, set your intention and be very clear about what you want to achieve. Don't simply say, "I want a job;" say something along the lines of, "I will get a new job in theater by the end of the year and I will be a success at it."

3. Next, cleanse your candle. As with crystals, cleansing helps to remove any negative energy the candle has picked up. To do this you can wave sage or incense smoke over your candle with a feather or by hand, bury it in sea salt for 24 hours, or leave it outside overnight when there is a full moon.

4. To dress your candle, apply a dressing oil to the sides with a cloth (avoiding the wick) that is aligned with your intention. If you want to bring something new into your life, dab the oil from the top to the middle, then from the bottom to the middle. If you want to let go of something, dab oil from the middle outward to the top and bottom.

5. To increase your magic, make sure you clearly state your intention as you dab the candle with oil, focusing on your goal and mentally pouring that vision into the candle.

Make your own dressing oil

Here is a recipe for some basic dressing oil for your candles. You need a 5 oz jar with a lid, some carrier oil such as coconut, jojoba, apricot kernel, sweet almond, olive, grapeseed, or sunflower oil, and a selection of fragrant herbs.

To make the dressing oil, first add 1.6 oz of the carrier oil, followed by 1.6 oz of herbs, and then a second 1.6 oz measurement of carrier oil. Put the lid on the jar and shake vigorously. Keep this in a cool, dark place and shake the jar twice a day to mix the ingredients.

BUILDING THE GRIMOIRE

There's no better way to collect your witchy magical thoughts, recipes, and plans together than in a grimoire! A grimoire is a fancy name for a witch's book. Grimoires can be full of spells, information on the different branches of witchcraft (such as tarot, crystals, spellwork, etc.,) and witchy tips and tricks.

WITCHCRAFT | Building The Grimoire

The joy of a grimoire

Most modern witches learn their craft from a lot of different sources, from any number of websites, blogs, and books on the subject—and from fellow witches. They read and learn some aspects of the craft that suit them, and some that don't. No two witches are the same. Most witches work by trial and error, or instinct, taking on the spells or rituals that work for or ring true to them, and ignoring or dropping the parts that don't gel. A grimoire is a great place to store the information, tools, tips, and tricks that you want to use in your practices for future reference. That way, whenever you forget the meaning of a crystal or color, or need a spell to conjure up some courage, you can open your grimoire and find exactly what you need.

Choose your grimoire

The first thing to do is decide what sort of grimoire you want to create. Some witches choose giant, ancient-looking books with parchment style paper to use as their grimoires. More modern-minded witches type up their notes and keep them in a document file. You can buy special journals to use as grimoires, use ring binders, or even scrapbooks. Many witches like to handwrite their entries in a sketchbook, so they can add sketches and make their calligraphy big and flamboyant.

Have fun with it

Get creative and make your grimoire a pleasure to see and hold. It's a book all about rituals and magic, so it should look spellbinding and mystical to you as well! There are so many ways to decorate a grimoire. You could press flowers and herbs between its pages, add stamps, photographs, stickers, or other embellishments. You could use border scissors to cut the edges of the pages into different shapes. Go to town on the cover. If you're big on crystals, you could even draw or attach smaller gems on the cover of your grimoire.

INTRODUCTION TO SPELLS AND INCANTATIONS

Have you ever made a wish while blowing out your birthday candles or knocked on wood for good luck? Then you, like most of us, have already used a ritual of some kind to try to make your hopes and dreams come true. A spell is basically just a special way of asking for something you want.

How spells work

Spell casting is a powerful way of focusing an intention to manifest a goal. They can help us become more focused and determined to get what we want. Most spells consist of three steps: creating an intention, invoking it through a ritual, and putting that intention into action. So, for example, you might decide you want to date that person you have a crush on. That's your intention. You invoke your intention through a ritual like a love spell. This spell helps you put your intention into action, like finally opening up that dating app, or finding the courage to text your crush.

Spells are powerful manifestations. When we go through the process of gathering ingredients, creating a sacred space, and performing spells, we feed the intention behind our wishes. This makes them stronger. Such spell casting might not look as dramatic and explosive as we see in films, but they're still quietly powerful!

Do it like you mean it!

Casting a spell is a great way to focus on what you want in life and set your intentions toward your goals, and some say the most important part of any spell is your intention. Your intention is critical to casting spells. Magic spells are used to increase the power of your mind and your control over that power. So, while spell casting is—and should be—fun to do, you also need to commit to it. Spells will only work if they're backed up with some real conviction and commitment.

Spell casting can take many forms, from candle burning, crystal gazing, incantations, rituals, and bathing. Get ready to dive into a variety of spells to begin your journey as a fledgling witch, but feel free to expand or adjust these spells as you see fit. There's no correct or incorrect way to make magic, and that's what makes it so special. You can choose to follow a spell to the letter, or use it as inspiration to create your own power-summoning ceremony.

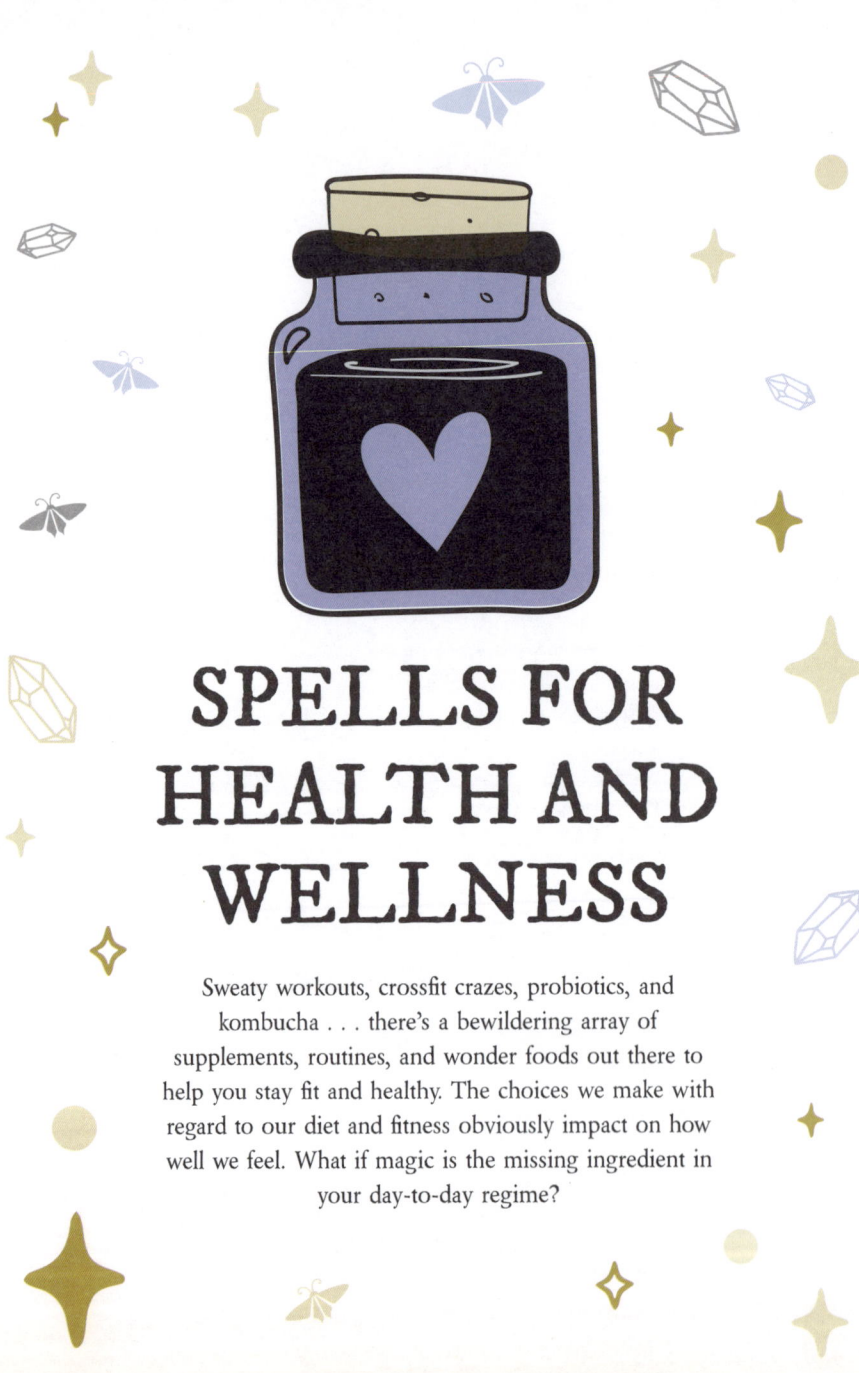

SPELLS FOR HEALTH AND WELLNESS

Sweaty workouts, crossfit crazes, probiotics, and kombucha . . . there's a bewildering array of supplements, routines, and wonder foods out there to help you stay fit and healthy. The choices we make with regard to our diet and fitness obviously impact on how well we feel. What if magic is the missing ingredient in your day-to-day regime?

WITCHCRAFT | Spells For Health And Wellness

Making magic

Magic spells for health and wellness take a variety of forms. The intentions and manifestations associated with spells are a great way to help you tap into that energy. Casting spells can help you take control of your health and wellness with a new glow of positivity, and they are a great way to replace lethargy with a fresh flow of enthusiasm. Herbs, spices, and other botanicals used in witchcraft can help, too. Plants can be used as incense, in the form of oils, or eaten as food to help us absorb their magical qualities. Our immune system is our body's first line of defence and protects us from both negative energy and unwanted bugs and germs, and one way to boost that immune system is with healing and protective medicinal herbs—ideal magic for health and wellness.

Take care of yourself

Spells help maintain health and wellness but like any magic, they must be backed up with real-world action. Spells and affirmations can also help empower you to follow a path of self-care and remain a well witch for good.

- Eating well and getting exercise benefits your appearance, your fitness, and your state of mind.

- Rest and relaxation matter.

- Be mindful. For total wellness, take care of what you allow into your head.

GOOD TO KNOW

Before you dive into the world of self-healing, a word of caution. Some of the spells you'll find in this section are designed to help with ailments such as headaches or colds. They include herbal and natural remedies that can have big health and wellness benefits, but remember to seek medical advice for any progressive and/or prolonged ailments. If you continue to feel unwell or you have any signs of a worsening condition, don't delay—book a doctor's appointment as soon as you can. Perhaps take a charm or crystal along with you for luck and protection.

Sleep Spell Jar

A good night's sleep possesses a magic all of its own. Making a sleep spell jar can also help you conquer insomnia, bad dreams, or regularly waking in the middle of the night.

You will need:

- A glass jar with lid
- Lavender
- Chamomile
- Passionflower
- Valerian
- Lemon balm
- An amethyst crystal
- A white candle

1. First, put on some soothing, peaceful music to get you in a restful mood while you make this spell jar. A recording of ocean waves or rain pattering would be ideal.

2. Light the candle. The color white can help to protect you from negative forces.

3. Place all your ingredients in your jar, one by one. As you add the objects to the jar, think about what your intentions are for your sleep and how you need this spell jar to help you. Add the amethyst crystal last. Amethyst will help you to drift into a deep sleep, reduce the risk of nightmares, and ease the effects of insomnia.

4. When the jar is filled, screw on the lid and seal it with molten candle wax.

5. Place your sleep spell jar beside your bed, where it can use its powers to give you a good night's rest. Gaze at it as you drift into the land of nod and focus on the benefits it will bring.

Good Health Spell Jar

This spell jar is a great remedy to make for yourself when you need a pick-me-up or as a preventative measure to keep you healthy and well.

You will need:

- A glass jar with a lid
- Rosemary
- Calendula
- Sage
- A daisy
- Black salt
- Small crystals for protection and luck, such as amethyst, rose quartz, or black obsidian
- A blue candle

1. Pick a quiet time and space, such as your altar, where you can be calm and undisturbed. You want an ample opportunity to really enjoy making your jar, to infuse it with good energy.

2. Gather together all your ingredients and place them in front of you. You don't want to interrupt the spell by having to run off to the kitchen to fetch something you've forgotten halfway through!

3. Put the ingredients in the jar, one by one, arranging them in a way that looks pleasing to you.

4. As you put the ingredients carefully into the jar, repeat an affirmation of your choice about your health. You could say something like: "I am fit and I am healthy," or, "My body has all it needs to be well."

5. Light your candle, screw the lid on the jar and seal it using some of the molten candle wax. It's important to seal a spell jar with candle wax in a color that represents your intention. Here you are using a blue candle for healing, health, and calmness. Repeat your intention as you seal your spell jar with the wax.

6. Put your finished spell jar somewhere you can see it and experience its energy often, like a bedside table.

Poppet Magic Healing Spell

Poppet magic uses a doll to represent the person on whom the healing magic is to be focused. Poppets are simple to make and it's a fun, creative, and caring spell to cast.

You will need:

- Two pieces of fabric, around 5 inches x 5 inches
- Glue or a needle and thread
- Chalk
- A pair of scissors
- Salt
- Chamomile flowers
- Vervain or lavender
- A black marker or some bandages
- Colored pens or thread for decoration

1. Lay two pieces of fabric on top of each other. Using the chalk, draw an outline of a simple body, a bit like a gingerbread man.

2. Cut out the pieces and stitch or glue them together around the edges, leaving an opening of an inch or two wide down one side.

3. Stitch or draw a face on your poppet. Get as creative as you like!

4. Use the hole you've left in the seam to add something inside the doll that represents you or the person you want to heal, such as a lock of hair or a scrap of fabric from their clothes.

5. Add the healing herbs and flowers to the inside as well and stitch or glue the opening closed.

6. Now the doll is complete, to intensify the healing powers of the herbs inside, you can draw a black circle on the poppet where the ailment is concentrated, or bandage the part that is hurt (for example, a broken leg).

7. Place the poppet on your altar, close your eyes, and visualize yourself or the sick person being in vibrant health.

8. Once the recipient of the spell is better, sprinkle salt on the poppet to separate it from the energy of the person it represented, and dispose of it.

WITCHCRAFT | Spells For Health And Wellness

Self-Healing Spell

This self-healing spell is designed to tackle emotional pain. This can mean anything from a broken heart, anxiety, stress, or any other emotional strain that is holding you back from wellness.

You will need:

- Pink cotton fabric square, around 5 inches x 5 inches
- Pink ribbon
- Willow leaf
- Spearmint
- Cinnamon
- Lavender
- Lemon balm
- Quartz crystal

1. Hold the quartz in your hands, close to your heart. Quartz is a great healing stone. You can use it to bring yourself back into balance or to amplify any positive intentions.

2. As you hold the quartz, let your heartache or worries rise to the surface. Cry if you need to. Try to let the pain out and let the quartz crystal absorb some of that negative, damaging energy.

3. Lie your pink fabric square on your altar. Pink is a good color choice for spiritual and emotional healing.

4. Place the willow leaf in the center of the fabric. Willow helps to overcome sadness and has healing properties.

5. Lay the quartz on the leaf and then sprinkle the herbs one by one in a circle around the crystal. These herbs help with protection, healing, mental clarity, and serenity.

6. As you sprinkle the herbs, state your intentions, either out loud or in your head. For example: "I am whole, I am well."

7. Gently fold the corners of the fabric over to wrap up the herbs, taking care not to spill any. Then you can roll the parcel into a scroll shape. Tie your fabric scroll up with the pink ribbon.

8. Sleep with this parcel under your pillow. When you feel better, you can dispose of the spell. You can scatter the herbs outside and cleanse the quartz for reuse. If you feel you might need to cast the spell again, wash and reuse the fabric square and ribbon, too.

SPELLS FOR PEACE AND HAPPINESS

Everything is energy. When you spend a day with someone who is negative, you can absorb some of that energy and return home feeling anxious and drained. When you spend a day with a bunch of fun, inspiring, and loving people, you walk away feeling refreshed and uplifted, like you can be and achieve anything because you've absorbed some of their positive energy.

Face your demons

Most of us are generally optimistic and have a "glass half full" attitude to life. We try to wake up and get out of bed with a positive frame of mind and feel grateful for the good things in our lives. However, there are lots of things that can bring us down. Bad news stories can make you feel depressed and helpless. An argument with a friend can leave you feeling emotionally bruised and fed up. Being rejected from a job or by a crush can knock your confidence and self-esteem. Whatever your problems, imagine what your life would be like without those worries. It's time to take action to tackle some of these demons. And one way to do that is with affirmations and spells.

Be the change

Magic spells and affirmations can go a long way in helping you find peace and happiness, but using this kind of witchcraft won't always prevent you from feeling pain or sadness in the future. So alongside spell casting and rituals, save some of your amazing energy to stay focused on managing your own thoughts, feelings, and behaviors. This way, you can cope with hurdles you meet along the way and leap over them more easily, so they don't form a barrier blocking your joy and serenity.

The following spells for peace and happiness can help you address some causes of stress and anxiety in your life. They can help you become a fulfilled, healthy, and happy person by helping you to create a harmonious home environment, and ward off work worries with stress-relieving spells. You will use crystals for calm and healing, and essential oils to conjure enchantments, and rituals for relaxation and letting go. You'll learn how to make soothing spell jars and more that you can call upon to help you rid your life of negative energy, creating space for positive vibes that will help you find peace and happiness.

Happiness Spell Jar

When it comes to making a happiness jar, it's best to get really specific about what items you choose that remind you of the kind of happiness you seek. The list below gives some ideas of things you could add to your jar, but be creative and find your own, if you prefer.

You will need:

- A glass jar with lid
- A photo of you from a day when you felt really happy
- A small piece of fabric from an old favorite top
- A crystal or two to bring happiness, such as citrine or peridot
- Wildflower petals
- Uplifting incense, such as ylang-ylang or patchouli
- A piece of paper
- A pen
- A yellow candle

1. First, clear your head with a few cleansing breaths or some meditation. Do whatever suits you to get into a positive headspace. Maybe put some calming music on in the background.

2. Light the incense to help you cleanse your space and feel at peace.

3. Add the photo, fabric, crystals, and petals to the jar one at a time, thinking about what each thing represents and how it relates to your intention.

4. Write down your intention on the paper. For example: "I will feel happy," or, "I am at peace."

5. Fold this paper three times and place it in the jar.

6. Light the candle and state your intention out loud or in your head. As you do this, visualize how your wish will feel when it comes true.

7. Screw the lid on the jar and seal it with wax from your candle.

8. Place your happiness jar somewhere you'll see it often to remind you of your intention, such as on a bedside table. Looking at it and focusing on the happiness you hope it will bring before sleep and on waking will help to focus its power.

WITCHCRAFT | Spells For Peace And Happiness

A Mind-Cleansing Bath

If you're feeling stressed, confused, or upset, it's sometimes hard to see how you'll rediscover those old feelings of peace and happiness. Making time for a long and relaxing, spiritual bath can help you to replace those negative feelings with tranquility, and clarity.

You will need:

- A glass jar
- 1 cup Epsom salts
- ½ cup coarse pink salt
- Sage oil
- Rosemary oil
- Geranium oil
- Rose oil

1. First, add the salts to the jar.

2. Then, measure out a total of 20 drops of essential oil. This should be made up of 8 drops of sage oil, 6 drops of rosemary oil, 3 drops of geranium oil, and 3 drops of rose oil. Add these to the jar.

3. Next, infuse your potion with positivity. To do this, simply hold your hands over the open jar of salts and oils and visualize love and positivity flowing from your heart, down your arms, through your hands and fingers, and into the potion.

4. Run yourself a hot bath and pour the potion into the bathwater. As you do so, focus your mind and energy on what the potion will help you to achieve. You could repeat this phrase or another of similar effect: "With this potion I infuse the water with tranquility and clarity, peace, and happiness."

5. Get into the bath and lie there quietly, with your eyes closed, absorbing the potion's power, and breathing in its spellbinding scents.

6. Stay there as long as you like, or until the bathwater gets cold!

Calming Spell Jar

If anxiety and stress is preventing you from enjoying peace and happiness in your life, have a go at making one of these calming spell jars. As always with spell casting, feel free to take or leave what you want from the following ingredients list. You can work with whatever calming ingredients you have in your witch's pantry if that is more convenient!

You will need:

- A glass jar with lid
- Dried chamomile
- Lavender or bergamot oil
- A bowl
- Water
- Crystals with calming powers, such as amethyst, celestite, or malachite
- Pink salt
- A purple or light blue candle

1. First, fill the bowl with water and sit it on a windowsill or outdoors (somewhere it can't be disturbed by cats or other animals) so it can bask in the light of a full moon. Let the moon charge your water overnight. Moon water has been used for centuries to help humans embrace and absorb cosmic energy from the full moon.

2. Next, place your herbs, a pinch of your salt, a few crystals, and a couple of drops of oil into your jar alongside your moon water. Do this one at a time and, as you put each item into the jar, think about the magical properties it contains, and how it will help you to chase away feelings of anxiety and stress.

3. Light your candle. A light blue candle represents peace, harmony, and tranquility. Purple candles are associated with royalty, wealth, ambition, divinity, wisdom, healing, intuition, and psychic ability.

4. Now, take a few deep breaths and inhale the spellbinding scent emanating from the oils and herbs in your jar. Feel their soothing and calming effect on your mind and body.

5. Next, screw the lid onto the jar and seal it with some of the candle wax. Place this jar on a bedside table or your desk to invoke calmness and peace and ward off stress and anxiety.

Banish Bad Feelings

Use this banishing spell to rid yourself of all kinds of bad feelings, thoughts, or memories that stand in your way of finding peace and happiness.

You will need:

- A smudge stick
- A stick or wooden spoon (about 6 inches long)
- A piece of cord (about 24 inches long, ideally black)
- A piece of paper
- A pen
- A black candle
- Your favorite black protection crystal

1. Gather all your tools and place the crystal on your altar in front of you. Burn the smudge stick to cleanse your space. Open the windows and doors to your altar room to let out any negative energy.

2. Sit quietly and mindfully and focus your intention on the negative emotion you want to banish from your life. Think about how good you'll feel once this emotion has been expelled from your body and mind.

3. Light the candle and continue to focus on your intentions. Imagine your focus burning as you look at the flame.

4. Write the problem you wish to banish from your life on your paper. Be specific. Wrap this piece of paper around your stick or wooden spoon.

5. Next, slowly begin to wrap the thread/string round and round the paper and stick/spoon as tightly as you can.

6. As you do this, imagine you are trapping that unwanted energy and it is leaving you. Feel the weight of this negative emotion leave your body. Feel your body relax.

7. When you reach the end of the thread/string, tuck it into itself so it won't unravel.

8. Place your stick somewhere you can see or find it to remind you of your intention.

SPELLS FOR POWER AND PROTECTION

Protection and power spells are forms of magic you can do to ward off negative energy and strengthen your inner power and self-belief. They can help you to cleanse bad forces from your life and give you confidence that you are safe from danger and negative energy.

Back it up

Obviously, protection and power shields need to be used wisely. You can't take risks just because you cast a protection spell. Magic spells don't and shouldn't replace other kinds of home security and self-protection. You need to be savvy about staying safe, too. Back up your magic with action. You know the drill.

- Avoid risk-taking, such as going on a blind date with someone you've only ever spoken to on an app, spending money you don't have, or driving over the speed limit.
- Be careful what personal details—including photos—you give out online, by phone or in real life.
- Keep your stuff safe and secure and try to avoid flashing expensive items and jewelery on a night out.
- Listen to your intuition and follow your best judgment. If your friends are making bad decisions, you don't have to follow their lead. Have the confidence to say no if anyone makes you feel uncomfortable about anything.
- Trust your instincts. If you ever feel threatened by a situation or someone, leave. Listen to your body—a fast, pounding heartbeat, and churning stomach are signs you feel unsafe.
- Letting someone know where you will be at all times is a smart move. And always make sure you have a fully charged phone before you leave the house. If you are ever faced with a risky situation or get into trouble, your family and friends will know where to find you.

Take back your power

Spells for power and protection help to awaken your inner strength. They help you believe you are not powerless when faced with other people's bad energies or the threat of loss or harm. You have the power to conjure up a forcefield to hold harmful forces at bay by casting a protection spell. Many protection spells work by creating a shield that keeps away evil forces and negative energy. Protection spells also work like banishing spells, which help you get rid of other people's negative energy, and stop it from impacting your life or the lives of others you care about.

Crystal Jewelery Charms

If you want to relax in the knowledge that you are safe from negative energy all day and every day, one of the best ways to do this is by wearing your protective magic.

You will need:

- Jewelery that contains crystals or charms that resonate with you and makes you feel powerful
- A piece of paper
- A pen

1. Jewelry is a great way to carry your power on you throughout the day. Choose from protective crystals such as obsidian, turquoise, or carnelian. Obsidian is a strong psychic protection stone that has powerful properties that will help to shield you against negativity. Turquoise helps to enhance communication and expression and can help you to speak up for yourself when you need to. Carnelian is thought to combat feelings of inadequacy and to increase physical energy. You could wear a combination of different crystals.

2. Find a quiet spot in your home or out in nature where you can sit comfortably.

3. Close your eyes and take some slow, deep breaths to calm your mind and connect with your thoughts.

4. Hold your jewelry in your hand, look at the crystal, and think of what it embodies.

5. Before wearing your chosen jewelry, infuse it with a powerful affirmation. You could say: "I am gracefully embodying courage as I show up for myself each day with confidence, empowerment, and self-love," or, "My positive energy is safe from harm because I control it."

6. Repeat your affirmation until you feel it in your heart.

7. Then, write your affirmation on paper and keep it in a spot where you can see and read it every day.

8. Put your piece of jewelry on. When faced with challenges or fears, you should be able to hold or touch your jewelry to connect with the affirmation and the protection it holds.

WITCHCRAFT | Spells For Power And Protection

Smoke Cleansing Spell

Smoke has long been used by people to protect themselves from negative energy to ward off bad intentions. Burning incense is another ancient technique used to cleanse a space. Cleansing energy with a smoldering smudge stick also works effectively.

You will need:

- Incense
- Herbs and leaves, such as frankincense, pine, cedar, sage, or rosemary
- A candle
- A fireproof tray or plate, or an abalone shell
- Twine or string

1. Gather a bunch of herbs you want to use to cleanse and protect your personal space. Wrap the twine around it to create your smudge stick.

2. Light your candle.

3. Set an intention before setting fire to your smudge stick. For example: "As I light this tool, please protect me from any negative energy that tries to hold me back from my path, my joy, my health, and my purpose."

4. Then light the smudge stick in the candle flame by holding it at a 45 degree angle and pointing the tip down toward the flame. Allow it to burn for 30 seconds, and then blow it out.

5. Place it on any heatproof surface such as a fireproof tray or an abalone shell.

6. Leave it to smolder and release smoke for about five minutes.

7. Alternatively, you can walk around your personal space, fanning the smoke all over, whilst focusing your mind on cleansing and clearing any negative energy. If you feel you personally are being affected by negative energy, you can fan the smudge stick around yourself.

8. Your cleansing ritual is now complete.

Protection Spells With Bells

Bells have been used for centuries to ward off evil spirits and cleanse negative energy from an area or space. As well as having a magical quality, bells of course have a practical purpose and will ring to alert you to unannounced visitors if placed on a door.

You will need:

- Small bells with loops to put ribbon through
- Cord or ribbon
- Thumbtacks

1. Cut a length of ribbon and use it to tie a set of small bells together. You could add a bow at the top or tie the bell string to a hoop. Get as creative as you like—after all, these bells can double as a decorative ornament in your home. Some people change the ribbons with the seasons or for different festivals.

2. Pin the set of bells to a door or hang them from a window. As you hang them, repeat these words:

    THIS SPACE BELONGS TO ME. ANY NEGATIVE OR THREATENING ENERGIES HAVE NO POWER IN THIS SPACE.

3. Some witches put their protective bells on both the inside and outside of their doors. The great thing about witch's bells is that they are magic hidden in plain sight—there's no need to have to explain their function to those who do not practice witchcraft if you don't want to.

4. Leave your witch's bells to work their magic but remember to take the bells down now and then to cleanse or replace them to keep their magic fully functional and strong.

Witch's Ladder For Power And Protection

A witch's ladder is a type of "knot" magic that can be used for a wide variety of purposes. They are commonly made by plaiting or knotting ribbon or cords together while incorporating other materials that represent a particular intention.

You will need:

- Three equal lengths of white, red, or black ribbon, at least 40 inches long
- Materials to weave into the ribbon (such as feathers, herbs, beads, crystals, or charms)
- Metal ring (optional)

1. Tie all three ribbons together at one end, or you can tie them to a metal ring.

2. Braid the ribbons together and weave in feathers and other items as you go along.

3. You should incorporate nine knots into your ladder. Some people like to tie a knot where they weave in a charm or other items to ensure it stays firmly anchored.

4. As you make the ladder, you imbue it with magical energy by keeping your goal firmly fixed in your mind and visualizing your intentions.

5. When the ladder is almost finished, recite this simple spell while touching each one of the 8 knots you have created, then tie the 9th knot as you say the last line:

> By knot of one, the spell's begun. By knot of two, the magic comes true.
> By knot of three, so it shall be. By knot of four, this power is stored.
> By knot of five, my will shall drive. By knot of six, the spell I fix.
> By knot of seven, the future I leaven. By knot of eight, my will be fate.
> By knot of nine, what is done is mine.

6. Now you can hang the ladder on a door, a curtain rail, or above your bed or desk to give you the power and protection you seek.

Freezing Spell

Is someone bugging you? This freezing spell is designed to help prevent toxic people from bothering or contacting you anymore!

You will need:

- A zip-lock freezer bag
- Water
- A freezer
- A piece of paper
- A marker pen

1. Pour water into the zip-lock bag until it is about two-thirds full. (When water freezes, it expands, so don't fill the bag to the top.)

2. Use the marker pen to write a clear, personal intention on the piece of paper. For example: "I hereby bind X (insert name of the person that's bothering you) to stop them from criticizing me in front of my other friends," or, "I refuse to let X bring me down and interfere with my happiness any longer."

3. Fold the paper three times and say: "I hereby freeze X and bind them from bothering me again."

4. As you do this, focus all your energy and attention on imagining the person removing themselves from your life, or imagine their words no longer having any negative power over you.

5. Put the paper into the bag, seal it, and put it into a freezer. Leave it there as long as you need to.

6. Once the problem is done with, you can, if you wish (and if you need space in the freezer!), remove the bag from the freezer and thaw out the water. Bury the paper in soil in a yard or plant pot and pour the water from the bag over the spot where the paper is buried.

7. You can use this spell as often as you feel the need to in order to ensure your home is safe and protected.

WITCHCRAFT | Spells For Power And Protection

Protection Spell Jar

With its tough, spiky leaves, holly seems to be a plant destined to be used for protection. In this spell jar, you will use holly to give you something concrete to focus on and to remind you to feel safe, powerful, and protected.

You will need:

- A glass jar with a lid
- A holly leaf
- Some parsley
- A black hematite crystal
- A black obsidian crystal
- A smoky quartz crystal
- Pine needles or pine cones
- A piece of paper
- A pen
- A black candle

1. Collect all of your items together on your altar before you start. Don't stress if you don't have all three of the crystals listed above. You can use any protective crystals you like.

2. Start adding the ingredients to the jar one at a time. Take your time doing this and as you add an item to the jar, think about what it represents, and how it relates to your intention in casting the spell.

3. Finally, write down your wishes and intentions on the paper. For example: "I am always safe in my home," or, "In my home I am shielded from harm." Then fold it and put it in the jar.

4. Light the candle, screw the lid on the jar, and seal it with molten wax. As you do so, state your intention out loud or in your head, and enjoy the reassuring feeling of security and safety washing over you.

5. When you're done, put your jar somewhere you'll see it often to remind you of your intention. You could keep the jar on your altar, beside your bed, on a windowsill, by your door, or any place that feels right to you.

SPELLS FOR FRIENDS AND FAMILY

Relationships are a huge part of our lives. They can be challenging, of course, but in the long run they are one of the most important things in life. Building healthy relationships with friends, family, and partners is good for you. When relationships are working well, your mood, mental health, and well-being are all positively impacted. When relationships fracture, it can impact every aspect of your life.

The relationship rollercoaster

Relationships with friends and family are likely to go through testing times and there will always be ups and downs. It's like being on a relationship rollercoaster. One minute you're laughing and the next you could be screaming! Sometimes people you care about will let you down and sometimes you'll let them down. It can feel like you do nothing but argue with a sibling or find it impossible to talk to a parent. What if a friend becomes a negative force in your life and starts to drag you down? Or perhaps a relationship you care about is breaking down because of neglect? Spells can help.

Making magic happen

Casting a spell can help you to focus on what you really want out of a relationship. If you're shy and find it hard to make new friends, magic can be a supernatural support. There are rituals you can follow to help you take care of and maintain existing friendships. Some spells are designed to reconnect friends and family who have distanced themselves and forgotten how it feels to have those vital, close connections. If there are people with whom you've had a disagreement or fight and you find yourself in a state of separation or rift, remember: these problems can hurt a lot, but they don't have to last forever. Magical intentions can help you heal those wounds.

Nurturing relationships

If you don't water that house plant, it'll die. Relationships are similar. They're a living thing. If you don't give them attention, they'll wither away! Magic can help, but it'll only really work if you back it up with some direct action. Here are some tips for nurturing friends and family to ensure those relationships go on nurturing you, too.

Making Friends Spell

Some people seem to make friends easily, but for others it's a challenge. This spell will help you to make and keep new friends!

You will need:

- A blank postcard
- A gold pen
- A bay leaf
- Clear sticky tape
- 1 foot of thin, gold ribbon

FOR MAXIMUM EFFECT, CAST THIS SPELL ON A SUNDAY OR WEDNESDAY, OR ON A NEW OR FULL MOON.

1. The gold pen symbolizes success. Use it to write your invocation for new friends on the postcard. Write it as if it's an ad you might see in a shop window. Write the word WANTED at the top in bold letters and, below that, a description of the kind of friends you're looking for. It should look something like this:

WANTED
KIND AND ADVENTUROUS FRIENDS WHO I CAN HAVE A LAUGH WITH. HONEST, TRUSTWORTHY, AND LOYAL FRIENDS WHO I CAN CONFIDE IN AND WHO LIKE ME FOR WHO I AM.

2. When you're happy with the wording, use the clear tape to stick the bay leaf to the postcard.

3. Gently roll up the postcard and tie the gold ribbon around it, like a scroll.

4. While holding the scroll in your hand, take a few moments to focus on how you will enhance your magic. Remind yourself of all your good and likeable qualities. Think of ways to put yourself out there to talk to and get to know people. Make a personal pact to always be yourself, be persistent, and never be too quick to quit.

5. Leave the scroll on your windowsill for 24 hours so that your message will be carried out into the universe. Then, put it somewhere safe in your bedroom.

Reconnect With A Friend Spell

This simple spell will bring back a friendship with a little candle burning ritual. It uses the powers of salt for luck, purification, and protection, and cloves, which are often used to help keep good friends close..

You will need:

- 7 cloves
- Sea salt
- A piece of paper
- A pen
- An orange candle

1. Light the candle on your altar or table. In this spell we're using an orange candle for balance, memory, sharing, and kindness. Lighting the candle symbolizes the rekindling of your lost friendship.

2. Write your full name and your friend's full name on the paper.

3. Put the 7 cloves and sea salt on top of the names.

4. Close your eyes and focus your mind on a happy memory of a good time you and your friend shared. As you bask in this happy recollection, point your index finger at the names to pass the positive energy from the memory into the paper, and repeat these words:

WITH MY FINGER AND THIS REFRAIN I ASK THAT WE MAY MEET AGAIN, OUR STRONG FRIENDSHIP WE'LL RENEW AND PAINS OF THE PAST WE WILL UNDO, SO IT SHALL BE.

5. Sit quietly for a few minutes, or as long as it feels right for you, meditating.

6. Then blow out the candle and watch its smoke carrying your request out into the universe.

7. Fold the paper 3 times and give it to your friend if you feel it would help. Or bury the paper in soil, in the garden, or in a plant pot.

Farewell Frenemy Spell

Have you got a friend who is more of a "frenemy?" If you do, then it's time to move on! Use your witchcraft skills to help you disengage from this toxic person.

You will need:

- Objects that are reminders of the relationship (avoid nonbiodegradable items, such as plastic, if you can)
- A box
- A fireproof tray or plate
- Rosemary
- A clove of garlic

1. Collect a variety of objects that remind you of the frenemy. For example, perhaps a card they sent you, a photo of them, or a ticket you got when you went somewhere together. Or it could simply be something that reminds you of them, like a piece of food they like to eat.

2. Put all of the items into the box.

3. If the objects will burn, take them outdoors, scatter them with some rosemary, and set fire to them in the light of the moon on a fireproof plate or tray.

4. If they're biodegradable, bury them with a clove of garlic in a plot at some distance from where you live or work.

5. At this point, if at all possible or practical, let this person know that you wish to discontinue this relationship. You don't have to explain or justify yourself. Avoid giving them a list of their faults and try not to get caught up in a conversation with them. Keep it polite, but firm and simple. Just say something like: "This isn't working. I no longer want to continue this friendship with you. No hard feelings, but please don't contact me again."

WITCHCRAFT | Spells For Friends And Family

Bickering Brothers and Scrapping Sisters Spell

If you and your sibling are constantly fighting, then this spell may be for you. But you need to stop squabbling long enough to persuade your sibling to help you cast this spell!

You will need:

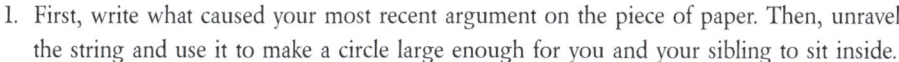

- A ball of string
- Two long pieces of white ribbon
- Two long pairs of different colored ribbons (say, two orange and two blue)
- A piece of paper
- A pen
- A bowl of rainwater
- A white candle in a candleholder

1. First, write what caused your most recent argument on the piece of paper. Then, unravel the string and use it to make a circle large enough for you and your sibling to sit inside.

2. Place the paper and all the other ingredients you need for the spell in the center of the circle and then you and your sibling should sit opposite each other. Light the white candle. Pick up a piece of white ribbon each. You should both sprinkle rainwater from the bowl on your piece while saying:

WHITE IS THE COLOR OF NEW DAWNS; WE HOPE OUR RELATIONSHIP CAN NOW BE REBORN.

3. Next, you each pick up a piece of colored ribbon that represents you and sprinkle rainwater on it while saying:

THIS IS MY WISH, MADE WITH ALL MY HEART.

4. Now, you each pick up a piece of ribbon that represents the other person and sprinkle rainwater on it while saying:

WE ARE TOGETHER BOUND BY POSITIVITY; WE COEXIST IN PERFECT HARMONY.

5. You should have three ribbons each now. Plait them together. Then each tie your plaited ribbon around your wrist. This represents your togetherness.

Family Harmony Spell

Is your family fractured by discord and friction? Are you ready to open the door to more harmony and happiness in your family? This spell won't prevent arguments or disagreements from ever happening, but it can bring a renewed sense of family unity into your life.

You will need:

- One pebble (or pieces of moonstone) for each family member
- Sea salt
- Water

1. First, dedicate each pebble in turn to a member of the family. To do this, hold each stone in your hand and say: "You are mother," "You are father," and so on. You can include as many family members as you like—even grandparents, aunts, and uncles.

2. Place the stones on your altar in positions that feel right. For example, family members who don't get along might be farther away from each other. Family members who have a good relationship might go closer together. It becomes a visual representation of where the distances and difficulties lie in the family.

3. Now gradually, stone by stone, move the pebbles into positions of unity, where they should be, such as parents together with children close by, until it looks more like a family unit.

4. Hold your hands over the pebbles and let love flow from your heart into all of them—even those who represent people with whom you have a difficult relationship!

5. Then, using your hands, gently begin to draw the pebbles even closer together until they all touch.

6. Close your hands over this family of stones and shut your eyes. Think about how important the love of this family is to you.

7. You can repeat this up to three times a day.

WITCHCRAFT | Spells For Friends And Family

Friendship Spell Jar

Make this friendship spell jar to attract, strengthen, and nurture close connections with people. This spell requires a number of ingredients, but each one is chosen to enhance and enrich the wish for meaningful friendships that you're putting out into the universe.

You will need:

- A glass jar with lid
- Sea salt
- Cloves
- A pinch of cinnamon
- Lavender
- A rose quartz crystal
- An amethyst crystal
- Dried dandelion
- A piece of paper
- A pen
- A teaspoon of sugar
- A yellow or white candle

1. On the paper, write down your intentions and wishes for this friendship. Try to be as clear as possible in your words. Say what you hope for in a friend or how you would like an existing friendship to grow and develop.

2. Charge your crystals for this spell. Hold each one in your hand, one by one, and imagine what you wish for and visualize a mind "movie" in which you watch you and your friend being happy.

3. Place both crystals on the piece of paper.

4. Fold the paper three times and then put it and the other ingredients into the friendship spell jar. As you put each ingredient into the jar, think about what it means, and how it will help you fulfill your desires.

5. Light your candle, screw the lid on the jar, and seal it with molten wax.

6. Place the jar by your bed or somewhere you will be able to look at it and think about what it means.

7. Remember that spell jars work best when followed up with intentions and an open heart that is ready to welcome new friendships, or strengthen present friendships.

SPELLS FOR LOVE AND SEX

Love is a little bit like magic. Both are all about possibilities—the possibilities of changing and enhancing your life. Both also require belief, courage, and commitment! Love spells are among the most popular of all spells cast, and no wonder, as so many of us are looking for romance, love, or even "The One," or struggling with heartache and mending a broken heart.

Love boundaries

Love spells can help you to find and improve loving relationships, but even the most powerful magic spells cannot force someone to fall in love with you. Love spells also need to be cast to manifest something that is within the realms of possibility. Any spell you perform needs to call upon a result that is reasonable and possible. In other words, you'll be wasting your time trying to cast a love spell on your favorite Hollywood celebrity! Love spells are mostly intended to be used to strengthen a connection with someone you already know and to help you enhance that connection. You also need to truly believe in your heart that the relationship can work. Positive intentions are key!

It's all about you

Even if you are looking for a spell to get the attention of someone you already vaguely know, it's still best to focus spells on yourself rather than on other people. For example, if what you need is to recover from a broken heart, casting a spell to get revenge on your ex might not work, while casting a spell to increase your self-love and worth might have more fruitful results.

As with almost all the spells you'll ever perform, the most important thing is not what you do, it's about how well you can focus, believe in, and concentrate on your intentions. It's not the crystals you choose or the candle you light, but the openness of your heart, and sincerity of your intention that you put into your love spells that will make them work. A little bit of patience doesn't go amiss either, as a love spell can take any length of time to work. It's hard to say how long the manifestation of a spell might take.

GOOD TO KNOW
There are many different reasons a love spell can miss its target, but if they really aren't working for you then maybe hit the pause button and have a think about what could be going wrong. Maybe you're not ready for new love? Perhaps you still haven't got over a broken heart? Or, maybe you always have the same issues that prevent you from opening up to a partner? Sometimes it can help to talk to a friend to work out if there are any deeper issues that are getting in the way of you finding love. Then again, maybe it's just not the right time for love for you. Take time instead to focus on work and other friendships and try again later when the time is more auspicious for you.

Manifest New Love

There are some love spells that you can do that require no ingredients at all. Instead, they depend on the magical power of manifestation. This love spell is designed to help you meet a potential partner or draw you closer to someone with whom you already have some kind of a connection.

1. First, check your lunar calendar. The best time to cast love spells is on a Friday because it's linked to Venus, the goddess of love, and on the day of a new moon, because these are symbolic of new beginnings.

2. On the appointed evening, settle yourself in a quiet room where you won't be disturbed and where you can fully relax and concentrate.

3. Set your intention. This is the most important part of manifestation, so be clear in your mind of what you'd like to achieve. Make your intention as specific as possible. The more clear and concise, the better. So, instead of saying, "I want to meet the partner of my dreams," focus on someone you already know and like, or come up with a detailed idea of what that person would be like, such as their personality, characteristics, and values.

4. When you're sure your intention is clear, focus on thinking about the person or type of person you wish to get closer to. Imagine being with that person, and imagine being in a loving relationship with them. Try to empty your mind of everything else, aside from the mental images you've created of the two of you together. Believe in the transformational power of your love and energy.

5. Repeat the manifestation once a month, ideally on the night of a full moon.

6. In order to see positive results, remember that while manifesting can help you turn your dreams into reality, you do need to help fate along by putting yourself out there and being ready and available to welcome new love.

WITCHCRAFT | Spells For Love And Sex

Romance Spell

When you have an infatuation with someone but they don't seem to have noticed it yet, this spell can help you feel love and romance in the air, and project the idea of the connection into the universe. With the right intentions, it should bring you and the object of your affection closer together.

You will need:

- A bathtub filled with water
- A glass of milk
- Some rose petals
- A rose quartz crystal
- Four new/unused, pink candles

1. First, take the time to give your bath a really good scrub. It should be cleaned and cleansed so the ingredients can work effectively.

2. Fill the bathtub with hot water and play some gentle background music to enhance the romantic atmosphere you are trying to build.

3. Stand a pink candle on each corner of the bathtub and light each one.

4. Pour the glass of milk, rose petals, and essential oils into the water. Place the rose quartz crystal in last, after charging it with your intention. Think about what you want your ingredients to help you achieve in order to fill them with magical energy.

5. Then, get into the bath, close your eyes, and relax. As you do so, be actively aware of the warm water flowing over your body and the romantic music.

6. Now, visualize yourself and the person you are attracted to as a couple. Picture yourselves together, being happy, and in love. Try to avoid thinking about anything else other than your intentions.

7. After soaking in your bath, collect the rose petals and dry them out. Keep them in your bedroom on a dish beside your bed.

Spell To Sweeten A Relationship

Are you and your partner having issues? This honey spell jar can help sweeten an existing relationship. Honey is often used in spells to bring two things together and is known to create balance, while the bee is a symbol of fertility.

You will need:

- A jar of honey
- A piece of paper
- A pen
- A boiled kettle
- A mug
- A teaspoon

1. Write the name of your loved one on the paper three times. The number three is significant here. For ancient philosophers, the number three was considered to be the perfect number; the number of harmony, wisdom, and understanding. It's also linked to Jupiter, the planet of joy, abundance, success, good fortune, and wisdom.

2. Next, write down your intention. This has to be expressed very clearly if the spell is to work. Be plain and concise. For example: "My love and I will listen more carefully to each other's needs."

3. Then, fold the paper three times, making sure that it fits neatly into the honey jar.

4. Take a spoonful of honey out of the jar and use it to make yourself some tea with freshly boiled water. While you drink and enjoy this sweet tea, repeat this affirmation: "As I take this tea, you'll be this sweet to me." You can say this aloud or in your head. You can also choose some words of your own to repeat at this stage.

5. Once you finish your tea, there is one thing left to do. Put the lid back on your honey jar and bury the jar somewhere safe. Ideally, find somewhere near some flowering plants or herbs, or at the bottom of a plant pot, fully submerged.

Spell To Get Over A Breakup

While falling in love can make you feel like you're walking on air, breaking up can sometimes send you crashing down again. Splitting up with a partner, whether it's a long term or a fairly new relationship, can leave you feeling bruised and sad. This spell can help to lift some of that pain and help you start to heal that wounded heart.

You will need:

- A smudge stick made from rosemary and sage
- A candleholder
- An uncooked, uncracked, clean, and room temperature egg
- A small, black candle

1. First, light the rosemary and sage smudge stick and then wave the smoke through your room to fill your space with positive energy. Take your time to do this slowly and rhythmically, taking in the smell and cleansing properties of the smoldering herbs.

2. Next, put the candle in the candleholder. Set it on your altar and light it. (You need a small candle because you want it to burn for a short time, just the length of time it takes to complete the spell.)

3. As the candle burns, take the uncooked egg and gently rub it over your body, taking extra time and focus over the heart area. Eggs are a symbol of life and they can draw negative energy out of your body. The egg should soak up your sadness and take it inside its shell. Think of the egg as a sort of psychic vacuum cleaner!

4. When the candle has burned out, take it and the egg, and dispose of them in a trash can, or bury them outside in the earth.

Note: it's natural to feel weary after this spell. Carrying sadness and negative energy is tiring, and letting it go is tiring, too. You should feel better and have more positive energy within a day or two.

Binding Spell

Happy in your relationship but every time you mention the word "exclusive," your partner runs for the hills? Perhaps what you need is a binding spell.

You will need:

- A photo of your beloved
- A photo of yourself
- A piece of parchment paper
- A pen
- Black thread or ribbon
- Rose oil
- A toothpick
- A fireproof tray or plate
- A small, pink candle

1. Take the toothpick and use it to gently carve your name and the name of the other person on one side of the pink candle. Then carve an image of a simple key on the other side of the candle.

2. Dress the candle by covering it with rose oil. As you dress your candle, say the words that describe your intention, for example: "With this pink candle, I'll infuse my relationship with commitment." Light your candle and repeat your intentions.

3. Next, write both your name and your lover's on the parchment paper, then carefully pour melting wax from your lit candle over the paper. The key thing here is to make sure that you cover both names with the wax.

4. Take the two photos and wrap them in the parchment paper. Tie the black thread or ribbon around the paper parcel with the photos inside. As the candle burns down, focus your mind on your intentions and desires.

5. After the candle has burned down, put the parcel of photos under your bed for a week. Then, take it out, burn it carefully (such as on a fireproof tray outdoors), and dispose of the ashes.

WITCHCRAFT | Spells For Love And Sex

Self-Love Spell

One of the most important forms of love is self-love. Loving yourself means taking time to look after yourself, being kind to yourself, and owning your thoughts and opinions.

You will need:

- A glass jar with a lid
- Rose petals
- Lavender
- Pink salt
- Lemon peel
- Sandalwood
- A rose quartz or clear quartz crystal
- A pink candle
- A piece of paper
- A pen

1. Write some self-love affirmations or self-love quotes on the piece of paper. Write them as beautifully and clearly as you can. This could include phrases like: "I accept myself for all of my beautiful and not-so-cool quirks and qualities," or "I believe that I'm capable of achieving and creating the life that I deserve and dream of," or, "I'm going to spend time with people who support, encourage, and motivate me to be the best version of myself."

2. Then, place the ingredients into the jar. Arrange them so they look appealing and enjoy taking your time doing this.

3. Light the pink candle, screw the lid on the jar, and seal it with molten wax.

4. Stand your self-love spell jar on your altar or bedside table, or somewhere else you will see it often, so it can remind you to practice more acts of self-love.

SPELLS FOR WEALTH AND PROSPERITY

The money and prosperity spells you'll find here are intended to help you find a level of wealth, prosperity, and success that equates to financial security, well-being, and good career opportunities.

Money matters

Before taking on these spells, have a think about your attitude toward money, and be honest with yourself; are you someone who tends to waste money? Wasting anything, including money, creates negative energy. If you continue to splash your cash on stuff you don't need, that's going to make it very hard to conjure up abundance and wealth, no matter how hard you try. On the other hand, worrying about money all the time and holding on tightly to all your cash will not bring you happiness, either. Like so much of life, it's all about balance—in this case, striking a balance between saving and spending. It's also a state of mind. Try to make your thoughts about money more positive. For example, on occasions when money is tight and you worry yourself with thoughts such as, "I can't possibly afford that," change your mindset to "I'd rather not spend my money on that right now," or, "My funds are just a little low at the moment."

TOP TIPS
Here are some tips for taking charge of your finances before you set up your spells. Some of it might sound obvious, but it's always good to remind ourselves of what matters most.

- Only spend what you can afford and cut down on wasteful spending. Don't spend what you don't have. Try to avoid getting into too much debt. The longer you take to pay a debt, the more you'll end up owing.
- Take some time to set a budget and track your spending. This involves working out what you've got coming in and what's going out, and making sure that you can afford all your bills and necessities. Once you've set yourself a budget, try to keep an eye on where you're spending your money.
- After you've got your budget pinned down, you can start to put some cash aside for unexpected emergencies. The idea of an "emergency fund" might seem extreme, but it's a way of making sure you've got some money on hand for an unplanned expense without falling into debt.

So, are you ready to manifest some money and make a dash for the cash? Just remember three things: first, take control of your ideas about money and any negative spending habits; second, be patient—as with any spell casting, you cannot control how long spells and manifestations will take; and finally, have faith in yourself and your ability to bring your dreams and desires to reality.

Passing Tests Spell

This simple spell is designed to help you pass a test with flying colors. (Of course, this will only work if you've also revised for the test or prepared for the interview properly, too!)

You will need:

- 1 incense stick or essential oil (such as lemon, lavender, rosemary, cinnamon, or peppermint)
- A piece of paper
- A pencil
- Your study books or course material
- A yellow candle

1. First, light your chosen incense or burn your essential oil. Place your hands on your study guides. Take three long, deep breaths. Relax and have a positive attitude. Meditating for a few minutes and absorbing the cleansing scent of the oils will help to ground you.

2. Draw a sketch of the sun on the piece of paper. This image can be as big or small, decorative or simple as you like. Just think about what you're drawing and be conscious of the way the pencil moves across the paper.

3. Light the yellow candle. As it burns, stare into the flame and chant this spell:

> I OPEN MY HEART TO THE POWER OF THE SUN,
> I SEE DEEP INTO THE GLOW OF ITS LIGHT,
> WITH ITS BRIGHT FOCUS AND WISDOM,
> I CAN PASS THIS TEST.

4. Imagine basking in the sun's light and feeling it clear your mind. You're invoking the sun's energy to give you strength, focus, and memory to help you pass the exam.

5. Meditate for a few minutes.

6. When you're done, blow out the candle but keep the drawing of the sun. You will need to take this with you to be your lucky charm for the exam, perhaps in a pocket or bag, or where you can see it on a desk or table.

WITCHCRAFT | Spells For Wealth And Prosperity

Money Spell Jar

To get the most out of the energy you're trying to attract into your life using your spell jar, you need to take action to achieve your goal as well. So, if you want to achieve more success or earn more money, you've got to put yourself out there and find a new job, a new course, or talk to people who can help you.

You will need:

- A glass jar with lid
- A jade crystal
- A green aventurine crystal
- Ginger
- Thyme
- A selection of seeds
- Rice or flour
- A piece of paper
- A pen
- A green, gold, or yellow candle

1. First, take a few cleansing breaths or cleanse the space around your altar in your preferred way.

2. Write down your intention on the paper and place it in the jar. You could write something like: 'Success and prosperity are coming my way', or, 'Money will be mine'.

3. Place your items in the jar one at a time. You really need to do this mindfully and with intention, thinking about what each object represents, and how it might help you achieve your goal.

4. Light a green, gold, or yellow candle (colors which symbolize success and prosperity) and state your intention out loud. As you state your intentions, imagine what it will be like when they come true.

5. Screw the lid on the jar and seal it with molten wax from your candle.

6. When you've finished the ritual, put your jar somewhere you'll see it often, to remind you of your intention.

Necklace For Success Spell

In this spell, you will fill a tiny, corked bottle or jar to hang on a necklace with herbs and spices from your kitchen that will help you attract money. Allspice is associated with money and good fortune and ginger calls forth prosperity and success!

You will need:

- A tiny, corked bottle or jar to hang on a necklace
- Allspice
- Ginger
- Ground or whole cloves
- Nutmeg
- Ground cinnamon
- A small funnel or folded paper
- A tiny piece or shavings of tiger's eye (or clear quartz)
- Bergamot oil
- A gold or yellow candle

1. Open your bottle/jar and use the small funnel or folded paper to help you pour some allspice, ginger, cloves, and nutmeg into it. These herbs and spices form the base layer of your spell.

2. Now, hold a tiny piece of tiger's eye or the shavings of tiger's eye in your hand and charge it with your intentions. Then, add it to the bottle/jar. Tiger's eye is good for luck and will add power to your spell.

3. Add some ground cinnamon, a botanical that not only helps you attract money and prosperity, but also intensifies the properties of the other herbs.

4. Sprinkle in a few drops of bergamot oil to attract success and encourage prosperity. It will also make your money spell necklace fragrant and more powerful.

5. Light a gold or a yellow candle as these colors correspond with luck and good fortune. Cork the bottle/jar and carefully seal it with wax from the candle.

6. Wear the necklace or keep it by you to work its magic and bring you prosperity.

WITCHCRAFT | Spells For Wealth And Prosperity

Find A New Job Spell

This spell will help you get the job you desire and soon you should have enough money in the bank to pay all those bills and hopefully fund some of the fun extras you've been daydreaming about!

You will need:

- A piece of green paper
- A gold pen
- 3 mint leaves
- A teaspoon of dried sage
- 1 gold or silver candle in a candleholder

1. First, draw a large pentagram (a powerful symbol made up of a circle with a five-pointed star inside it) in the center of the piece of paper with your gold pen. Green and gold colors bring luck and money.

2. You now need to write the word "JOB" in the center of the star. Before putting pen to paper, make sure that the star is pointing up, not down, and don't make the word too big as you need room to add other words to the pentagram, too.

3. In the space around "JOB," write some other words describing your ideal job. Do you want an office-based or home-based role, outdoor work, or full or part-time work?

4. Rip the mint leaves into pieces and put them and the dried sage into the pentagram.

5. Sit the candleholder on top of the herbs and light the candle. Then repeat these words:

    NATURE AND THE UNIVERSE,
    I CALL ON YOU TO FIND ME A JOB I'LL LOVE TO DO,
    OFFER ME WORK TO PAY MY BILLS,
    AND ALL MY NEEDS AND WISHES ARE FULFILLED.

6. Wait for the candle to finish burning. Then remove the candle and carry the paper with the herbs resting on it to an open window. Blow the herbs out into the air to carry your intentions into the universe.

WITCHCRAFT LEXICON / INDEX

AFFIRMATION: The assertion that something is true, it exists, and you believe in it.

ALTAR: The workspace on which a witch performs their rituals and spells.

AMULET/TALISMAN: An object which has been ascribed magical powers, or with which intentions have been set. Amulets are natural objects, and talismans are human-made objects.

BOTANICALS: Plants or plant parts which can be used in spells for medicinal or magical purposes.

CHARMS: Objects which represent a change or result you desire, often carried around by the user, and believed to bring luck.

CRYSTALS: Crystals are naturally-formed minerals that can hold energy and are said to possess healing and protective properties.

DRESSING THE CANDLE: A method of charging a candle by applying essential oils to prepare it for use in magic.

ELEMENTS: Witches often work with the powers of the four elements of nature, Earth, Wind, Fire, and Air, in their craft.

ESSENTIAL OILS: Highly concentrated compounds extracted from flowers, herbs, roots, or resin and combined with carrier oils for use in various types of rituals, medicines, and therapies.

GRIMOIRE: A book of spells, rituals, and magical information.

INCANTATION: A series of words or phrases recited during the casting of a spell.

PENTAGRAM: A five-pointed star, often used as a magical or mystical symbol.

POPPET: A doll which is made to represent a person, to be used during spell casting to help heal or aid them in some way.

RITUAL: A set of actions performed in the hope of bringing a desired outcome or intention.

SPELL: A spoken or enacted ritual performed with magical intentions to bring about change for the user or someone close to them.

SMUDGING: A method of cleansing a space by burning a bundle of herbs, extinguishing the flame, and wafting the smoke around to rid the area of negative energies.

WITCH'S BELLS: A small bundle of bells which act as a traditional method of protecting the home from evil spirits and intruders. The bells are hung from doorways and windows.

WITCH'S LADDER: A magical tool made from knots of ribbon and other meaningful items which are braided together and hung in the home for power and protection.